Only Love Can Save Us

BaBa Angel

Balboa Press books may be ordered through booksellers or by contacting:

Balboa Press
A Division of Hay House
1663 Liberty Drive
Bloomington, IN 47403
www.balboapress.com
1 (877) 407-4847

ISBN: 978-1-9822-0721-2 (sc)
ISBN: 978-1-9822-0720-5 (e)

Library of Congress Control Number: 2018907359

Print information available on the last page.

Balboa Press rev. date: 06/26/2018

PRESS
A DIVISION OF HAY HOUSE

Foreword

In this book are messages/quotes from the ascended masters (Kwan Yin, Buddha, Jesus just to name a few) to the human race on how to heal ourselves as well as the planet in a world that desperately needs healing. With self-love and love for others and the planet we can do this together one person at a time – we become one. Hence, **ONLY LOVE CAN SAVE US**.

In truth and spirit, we are already there/here!

We must come to realize that our ultimate joy and happiness has and always will come from within, and that our solution is always unconditional love for self and others.

I love you Humanity, BaBa Angel and Ascended Masters.

Quotes from The Messenger
Ba Ba Angel

For God the Mother so loved the world that She sent into its midst the Divine Girl-Child whoever believes in her goodness, listens to her wisdom, and celebrates her power will be awakened to their abundant giftedness as a child of life. John 3:16

I overcame my hesitation to communicate new ideas to the world for that is what I have come here to do. Living for a purpose that is greater than yourself is what ultimately brings the greatest joy and satisfaction.

A messenger-Baba Angel

I am a figment of your imagination
And you're a figment of my imagination

If you want to change the
World start within yourself

A lack of self- love is the root of all suffering.
Self - love sets us free

Silence is purifying to the spirit.

I'm not on the floor anymore (in darkness) for my spirit has
soared to new heights of light (awareness)

Give love but you may not always get love so don't take it personally.

We are all one in spirit, but not always in sync at the heart level.

I am powerful beyond measure.

Only I have the power to determine the course of my day.

There are no coincidences only synchronicities.

The body is just a ray of energy that is affected and reflected by our thoughts.

The universe is divine orderly not chaotic

Providence moves in our favor when we are open to it.

Blissful, harmonious states within produce miracles without.

The body is in constant flux (not solid) meaning 98% of atoms in your Body will be replaced by new ones by the end of the year.

Adversity is the universe's way of teaching us lessons we need to learn.

Art generally raises the vibration of all who witness it.

Compassion is love in action.

Hope lies in our destiny of light at our core.

When you glow, it will show

The spirit is age-less, the body, no so much but it houses the spirit so it is oh so holy.

Make your life a prayer in the moment.

Silly and goofy that's me, saints were willy, nilly silly.

Love, God/Goddess and the power of the human mind
will make all things new.

Having to shift your energy from positive to negative is
more stressful than being consistently negative.

Laughter is healing to the mind, body and spirit.

Einstein proved that 99% of reality is invisible thought and spirit and only less than 1% form which is not solid but 99.9999999% empty space.

I am Goddess energy and no one can stop me now.

Ecstasy bliss come to the peaceful mind.

Love unconditionally the tiniest insect to the
whole of humanity

It's not can I – it's who is going to stop me.

All paths lead to the same place- God/Goddess
realization and unconditional love.

Nobody is right and nobody is wrong. We are all right
and we are all wrong simultaneously.

My life is a symphony of events that nourish my soul
Yoga, music, prayer, artwork, exercise, vegan food,
meditation, singing, dancing, writing, and volunteering.

You alone have the power to make yourself happy

They say, "We have a heart as big as the universe."

You can't miss what you already have.

Integrate the shadow and you become light and playful.

Contributor/distributor to the
birthing of a new reality on planet
earth Ascended Master to be – WE!

LOVE - voted most likely to save
the world one person at a time.

I know nothing and I know
everything

Gratitude is the latitude for unspeakable joy.

Resistance causes suffering, acceptance joy.

The universe calls us to express ourselves as light, love, laughter, compassion and beingness joy, peace and sereneness no matter what the circumstances.

It is a transformative process that moves us from darkness to light.

Wake up and start focusing on cures rather than fears.

Give negativity nothing to oppose and it will vanish on its own.

Remove the fear that is blocking your peace and serenity by focusing on the love energy (light) at the center of your being.

To manifest a higher vibration each is called but not everyone answers the call.

Aliens among us are anchoring light, wisdom and a higher consciousness. Is this an alien parking space?

Beyond our thoughts
bliss happens

Only I have the power to
appreciate myself.

I am the Goddess in
nature and no one can
stop me now.

Words get lost in the translation. It is in the silence (stillness) that God/Goddess communicates.

If it ain't fun why bother?

The world treasures the gift of gab (as a gift) while silence not so much.

Success is disguised as failure.

Silence is a girl's best buddy.

My three best friends: God, Goddess and myself.

On the path with
the Goddess to
gardens of Delight.

Even stars expire, some
forming supermassive black
holes of intense gravity pockets
where light cannot escape with
masses equal to 10 billion suns.
(Earth and sun also expire)

The secrets of the universe can
be unlocked from within (every
cell of the body)

Laughter is music
that spring from
within the soul (spirit)

My life is filled to over flowing with
indescribable unceasing magic.

The destiny of the world is in
your hands - God/Goddess

Store up your treasures on the inside because on the outside they can vanish.

Cosmic victory belongs to those who persevere.

Don't worry about tomorrow you may not make it.

Who knew (new) "Salvation" is here and now, not after you bow (out)?

Organized religions been there done that! Church of the heart is where it's at.

We are all drops in an ocean of love and gratitude.

Love is a ripple that can spread throughout the universe one drop at a time.

Thoughts and words have power - they attract energy.

An enormous ocean of love and
gratitude ripples across the universe.

You can't miss what you already have.

Beware! of the mind.

It takes creativity to find positivity.

The goddess showeth the way to those who can find it not.

Persistence breeds seeds of power.

Get out of your own way and let divine flow
show you it's way

Let go, let love flow

The green flash of the sun setting inspires
mindfulness (moon bow inspires the same)

A UFO uses tornados to harvest energy (who would' a thunk it)!

Goddess/Mother nature don't cause disasters, adversities or obstacles, karma and the human mind do. They only send us love to overcome.

I (ego) is an illusion, only love is real.

Do cast last your pearls before swine (those who don't understand) because eventually they will.

The way that is paved with miracles is the way of the heart.

Persist and you will find the "pearls of great price" that lies beyond our thoughts.

Reality is in the eye of the beholder.

I am an artist's pallet in expression.

Unbridled energy. In the void.

A moon bow rainbow sends the Goddess/God's love
in pastels of light across the sky.

There is no external heaven or h_ _ _. Each is an inner
state of mind (being).

Pro-peace, not anti-w_r.

There are as many paths as there are people (7.6 billion to be exact). Each one is significant.

When ignored, mistreated or unloved, don't take it personally - it's about them not you.

I am not a body or a name. I am a brilliant ray of the Goddess energy.

Goddess energy is power.

It's always working even when it's not working (divine order).

In Goddess's perfect timing love will prevail.

Nope not now but maybe down the road!

If things get in my way I can use two feet to walk away.

Gray (without) outside sunshine within

Count your options.

Self-actualization is an inside job.

We can love planet love into existence by the power of the mind.

These are at the heart of all religions, paths and practices
-Unconditional love and forgiveness for self and others 24/7
-Love one other as I have loved you
-Love yourself as your neighbor
-The kingdom of heaven is within
-We are all ONE in spirit

We always want to know what we know before we know it.

By using the creative power of the universe and mind each of us has the potential to change the world in an instant.

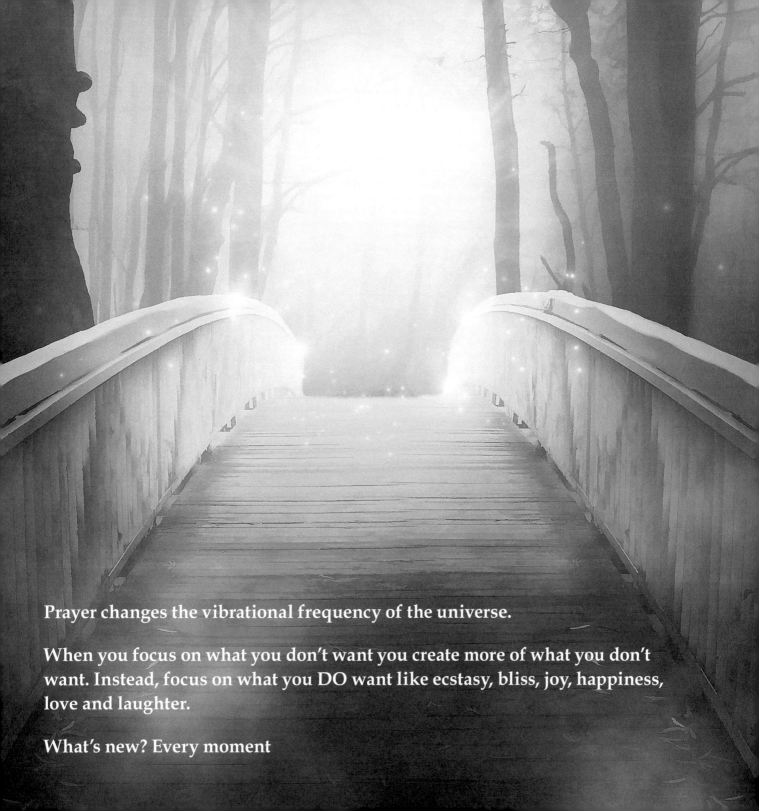

Prayer changes the vibrational frequency of the universe.

When you focus on what you don't want you create more of what you don't want. Instead, focus on what you DO want like ecstasy, bliss, joy, happiness, love and laughter.

What's new? Every moment

In the Goddess's eyes, we are all precious sparkly beings of light.

I am a figment of your imagination and you're a figment of my imagination

Silence is purifying to the spirit.

If you want to change the world, start within yourself.

My 4 best friends, the Goddess, me, myself and I.

Only you can love yourself.

Love all that is and isn't.

When falsely accused, release in love.

Embrace the present moment as a loving gift from the Goddess.

Now. It doesn't get any better than that!

Happiness is a choice and those who choose love are happy.

All the answers will be questions. The question is your answer.

How to stay centered and open-hearted amidst trials:
  1.) Step back
  2.) Observe
  3.) Detach
  4.) Accept that he/she has a right to their own behavior
  5.) Let go
  6.) Forgive
  7.) Love back
  8.) Pray

Gratitude is the attitude.

There are no sins or mistakes-only lessons.

Laughter, Joy, Love-natural age defyers

Cluttered mind, cluttered reality.

If you want to change the world, start within yourself

Think less. BE more.

A lack of self-love is the root of all suffering. Self-love sets us free

Forging new territory of the mind-alone.

All form is impermanent, only love lasts.

The body, the planet and the indescribable universe are all in the void of 99.9999999% empty space, which means the b—t and b--bs aren't real after all! Oops! It's the senses that make them seem real.

We're here to enjoy, celebrate and have fun despite circumstances.

When mistreated or falsely accused, count it all joy!

Only Goddess's love, spirit, and the infinite are real and form is only an illusion.

Savor the moment it only comes around once!

Splendor in the moment.

Love is eternal. We are eternal.

A psychotic is a gal who really gets it!

Savor the moment it only comes around once!

My sanity, hair today → gone to Maui.

Metta, Metta, Metta (loving-kindness meditation) is Betta, Betta, Betta.

She who laughs enjoys the fruits of her joy, which is contagious.

We are all on an incredible adventure of love that never ends.

The only judgment is that which we do to ourselves. NOT Goddess. She exists only as love, for Goddess and love are synonymous.

I won't let another person or the weather determine the course of my day.

Rain or shine, I'm just fine. Have a liquid sunshiny kind of day! Yeah!

Don't hope for peace. BE peace.

Be the love you wish to see in the world.

The only heaven or h--l you go to is the heaven
or h--l you take with you!

Love all that is and isn't.

Heaven exists only as love in the present moment.

Gratitude is the attitude

The material things in life don't last. Only love lasts.

I am an ageless magnificent, brilliant, being of light and so are you.

Printed in the United States
By Bookmasters